A *Doonesbury* Book by

G.B. Trudeau

The Thrill Is Gone, Bernie

Selected Cartoons from
UNFORTUNATELY, SHE WAS ALSO WIRED FOR SOUND
Vol. I.

FAWCETT CREST • NEW YORK

The Thrill Is Gone, Bernie

ISN'T ZONKER COMING DOWN FOR BREAKFAST?

HE'LL BE DOWN. HIS TRAINER JUST WENT UP TO GET HIM.

HIS TRAINER?

BERNIE. EVER SINCE HE HELPED ZONK WIN THE JACK FORD TANNING AWARD, HE'S BEEN FANATICAL ABOUT KEEPING HIM ON HIS SCHEDULE!

WELL, SKIP, THANKS FOR DROPPING BY..

HEY, GIVE THEM A CHANCE! IT'S BEEN TEN YEARS!

GBTrudeau

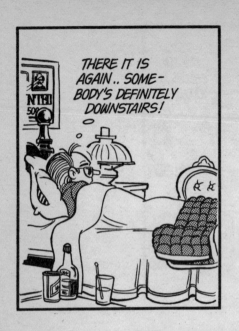

ANY NEW DETAILS, HONEY?

WELL, DUKE WAS ARRAIGNED YESTERDAY. THE JUDGE HAS SET THE BAIL AT $5,000.

"AS THE FORMER AMBASSADOR WAS LED FROM THE COURT-ROOM, HE LOUDLY DENIED ALL RESPONSIBILITY FOR THE SHOOTING OF EX-HANDYMAN ZEKE BRENNER."